Confidence

28 Killer Actions to Boost Your Self-Confidence

© Copyright 2019 - All rights reserved.

This document is geared towards providing exact and reliable information in regards to the topic and issue covered. The publication is sold with the idea that the publisher is not required to render accounting, officially permitted, or otherwise, qualified services. If advice is necessary, legal or professional, a practiced individual in the profession should be ordered.

- From a Declaration of Principles which was accepted and approved equally by a Committee of the American Bar Association and a Committee of Publishers and Associations.

In no way is it legal to reproduce, duplicate, or transmit any part of this document in either electronic means or in printed format. Recording of this publication is strictly prohibited and any storage of this document is not allowed unless with written permission from the publisher. All rights reserved.

The information provided herein is stated to be truthful and consistent, in that any liability, in terms of inattention or otherwise, by any usage or abuse of any policies, processes, or directions contained within is the solitary and utter responsibility of the recipient reader. Under no circumstances will any legal responsibility or blame be held against the publisher for any reparation, damages, or monetary loss due to the information herein, either directly or indirectly.

Respective authors own all copyrights not held by the publisher.

The information herein is offered for informational purposes solely, and is universal as so. The presentation of the information is without contract or any type of guarantee assurance.

The trademarks that are used are without any consent, and the publication of the trademark is without permission or backing by the trademark owner. All trademarks and brands within this book are for clarifying purposes only and are the owned by the owners themselves, not affiliated with this document.

Table of Contents

Confidence 1

Introduction 5

Chapter 1: 10 Insanely Effective Mental Actions That Boost Your Self-Esteem 6

Chapter 2: 6 Foolproof Health Actions that Effectively Improve Your Self-confidence 16

Chapter 3: 7 Highly Actionable Body Language Actions For Improved Self-Confidence 20

Chapter 4: 5 Super Powerful Confidence Habits You Should Adopt 26

Conclusion 29

Introduction

I want to thank you and congratulate you for purchasing the book, "**Confidence:** 28 Killer Actions to Boost Your Self."

Your faith and belief in yourself and your capabilities is one of the most important success factors. When you believe in your ability to do something, you are likely to stick to its pursuit until you achieve success.

On the other hand, when you lack faith in self, you are likely to harbor an inferiority complex that keeps you from pursuing worthwhile endeavors that have the potential to change your life as well as the lives of your loved ones and friends.

Fortunately, confidence is not innate, something granted to some and—and not others—at birth. Confidence is a learnable trait, something we can cultivate by the implementation of a few key strategies and actions.

In this guide, we discuss 28 select actions that when practiced consistently, have the potential to boost your self-confidence to levels never before imagined.

Thanks again for purchasing this book. I hope you enjoy it!

Chapter 1: 10 Insanely Effective Mental Actions That Boost Your Self-Esteem

Our beliefs shape our lives. If you believe that you are capable, you automatically reinforce this belief, and if a challenge comes your way, you are likely to seek solutions rather than let it defeat you.

Your mental attitude is one of the most significant parts of your self-esteem and faith in your capabilities. When your mental attitude is positive—albeit realistic especially in relation to what you can and cannot do—you are likely to have a strong faith in your capabilities and more importantly, in your ability to learn how to do everything well.

On the other hand, when your mental attitude is negative, you are likely to have a static belief of your ability to learn and grow.

To ensure you are consistently developing your self-esteem, here are several mental actions you can implement:

1: Become Mindful and Aware, A NOW Person

Self-awareness is the secret to all forms of personal growth. When you become aware of your strengths and weaknesses, it becomes easier to play to your strengths and to work on your weaknesses.

The most effective way to become self-awareness is to practice the art of mindfulness, i.e. become someone who revels in the present moment, the NOW. Life happens in the present moment. Oftentimes, however and unfortunately, we are constantly rehashing the past or planning for a future we know not what it will bring.

While there is nothing wrong with reminiscing and planning, letting these actions consume your mind breeds what researchers call a *Monkey mind*, a phrase of Chinese origin (shin'en 心猿) that means a mind that concerns itself consistently with what ifs, and therefore becomes unsettled, and according to Wikipedia, *"restless, capricious, whimsical, fanciful, inconstant, confused, indecisive, uncontrollable."*

On the other hand, when you become mindful of the present moment, a NOW person, you learn how to calm the incessant chattering of the mind, which when you do, instead of the mind concentrating on playing out "what if" scenarios, you start concentrating on how to live your best life in the present moment.

Moreover, when you become mindful and present, you become aware of your flow of thoughts, and because of it, it becomes easier to notice, and where necessary, let go off or replace negative thoughts with positive ones, an undertaking that helps you increase your confidence and build a positive thought pattern.

2: Positive Thinking

As noted, when you believe yourself to be a capable person, someone capable of learning and growing, you automatically increase your self-esteem. When you believe in your ability to learn and grow, no problem, challenge, or setback will devastate you to the point of giving up. Do you know why?

Because when you believe in the moldable nature of the human personality and mind, it affirms in you the belief that you are always a single lesson away from learning how to do something well. Coincidentally, the more you practice something, the more skillful you become and the higher your confidence in your capabilities soars.

How do you practice positive thinking especially in a way that builds your self-esteem? The easiest thing to do here is to practice positive self-talk. Whenever thoughts of your perceived inabilities flair up, counter them with positive thoughts that reinforce your ability to learn, grow, and perfect certain skills.

For instance, if a thought such as "I suck at building relationships" invaded your mind and causes you to shy away from engaging with fellow party attenders, counter it with a positive thought such as "talking to people and creating rapport is a learnable skill. If I talk to enough people, I am sure that I too shall master it."

By practicing positive thinking, or rather, positive self-talk, you effectively rewire your mindset to one that illuminates your capabilities instead of one that focuses on your inabilities and shortcomings. Doing this alone will have a profound effect on your level of self-confidence.

3: Practice Affirmations

This strategy is very similar to the one above it in that both relate to rewiring your patterned thoughts into positive ones. In this case, however, you closely watch your thoughts, and upon noticing thoughts that reinforce a negative self-image, you replace them with positive thoughts that improve your self-image and therefore self-esteem.

Here is an example.

You walk into a café and you notice a beautiful woman you would like to talk to. Before you take the plunge though, a voice inside your head says, "Look at her! She's the most beautiful woman you have ever seen! What makes you think she'll give you the time of day?" This is the voice of your negative thought.

If you take up the habit of being mindful of the present moment, you will notice that a large percentage of your daily thoughts consist of negative thoughts that when courted and welcomed to take up space in your mind, breed other thoughts that erode your self-confidence and form negative thought patterns and beliefs.

As you become mindful and take to the habit of observing your thoughts as they come and go, you will develop the invaluable skill of being aware of when negative thoughts flare up and keep you from seizing the moment. In the above instance, the thought breeds from an inferiority complex.

In such an instance, by being consciously aware of your moment-to-moment thoughts, you can use awareness to rewrite those thoughts into positive ones that help grow your confidence and motivate you into taking action.

In this case, when the negative voice flairs up, you can watch it nonjudgmentally and once it passes, speak to yourself positively perhaps by saying, *"We meet people for a reason. The universe has placed her in my path for a reason. I will say hello and engage her in a genuine conversation for I know not where it may lead."* Such a thought statement is likely to give you a jolt of confidence and motivation to seize the moment.

Other confidence-infusing affirmations you can use include:

"I am confident."

"I am worthy."

Find more affirmation from this resource:

In addition to using positive affirmations as replacements for negative thought and thought patterns, also chant positive, confidence-building affirmations as you go about your day, or at the least, three times a day: morning, lunchtime, and in the evening. The effect on your level of confidence shall be astounding.

4: Visualize

As you may have noted, the actions in this chapter specifically relate to helping reshape your thought patterns by attuning them to self-confidence. Of all the strategies you can use to improve your self-image, visualizing yourself as you want to be is the most effective and perhaps the easiest to implement for all it asks of you is to picture yourself as you want to be, which in this case is confident.

If you are about to take to the stage, visualize yourself as a confident speaker and you will be one. If you are about to take the plunge and talk to that beautiful woman, picturize yourself as a confident, attractive, and interesting man that women find irresistible; in everything you do, picture yourself as successful.

Holding a vivid mental image of yourself as the person you envision yourself to be and consistently work towards being has a profound effect on your confidence as well as your personality.

Moreover, by power of law, we attract into our lives that which we court mentally and infuse with emotions. When you create a vivid, emotion-laded picture of yourself as you want to be, in this case confident and worthy, you automatically start attracting circumstances and life experiences that reinforce this mental attitude: essentially, by picturing yourself as confident, you become confident.

5: Exercise Your Mind

It is important to point out here that a lack of confidence is a self-image problem that comes from the belief that you are incapable of doing something successfully. Think about it for a moment.

When you believe that you "suck at talking to women," you are likely to believe that your inability is innate and because of that, there is very little you can do about. When you believe yourself to be a bad public speaker, in the belief that you suck, you are likely to shun all public speaking instances that come your way.

One of the easiest and most potent ways to grow your level of confidence in your skills or abilities is to learn more about specific aspects of your life, what we are calling exercising your mind.

If you know you are not a very confident speaker, find, observe/read, and absorb quality content on the matter. If you consider yourself bad at speaking with women, it is reasonable to conclude that by consuming content that teaches you strategies relevant to "picking up" and flirting with women, your skill level will grow and so will your belief in your capabilities.

The more you learn and improve your abilities, the more confident you feel and become. When you notice an inferior complex relative to a certain area of your life, earnestly take up learning about how to improve in that area. How effective a strategy this turns out to be will amaze you.

6: Meditate

Meditation is a highly effective practice that can help you overcome an inferior complex and start improving your self-confidence. As you read this guide, keep in mind that self-confidence is your self-image, the image and belief you have about yourself and your capabilities.

In specific relation to building confidence, meditation is a very effective way to stop negative self-talk. As we mentioned earlier, your mental chatter creates your mental attitudes and mindset. If this mental chatter is predominantly negative, it will create a negative mindset; a negative mindset is not complimentary to a healthy level of self-confidence.

Meditation helps you quiet negative mental chatter and in so doing, it allows you to become present in the moment, reduce feelings of anxiety and insecurity, and limit self-defeating, self-destructive thoughts that steal your focus and continually chip away at your confidence.

When you take up habitual meditation, it becomes easier to stop negative self-talk. In addition, scientific research has indicated that by meditating, you improve your EQ, the ability to control your emotions, and your social self-confidence. All of these have the effect of greatly improving your level of self-confidence.

7: Decisiveness

Decisions are very characteristic of the human life. To build your confidence, become a decisive person. Make decisions fast but even as you do so, think your decisions through.

Here is the thing, the more you think about something, the more options you give yourself and guess what, the more options you have at your disposal, the harder it becomes to make a decision and the further your confidence to make one erodes.

Always remember that our abilities and capacities develop out of consistent practice. When you make quick decisions, you teach your mind how to think on its feet, which greatly improves your belief in your abilities.

Moreover, as you train your decision-making muscle and it grows, you will start making better decisions and because of it, you will start feeling more confident of your ability to make sound, well thought out decisions related to all areas of your life.

Here, we advise that you become decisive with smaller, inconsequential decisions and then work your way up to the big decisions.

8: Stop the Comparison Game

We habitually compare our lives—and ourselves—to the lives of our friends, acquaintances, people in the same age group, as well as people we interact with on social media and the internet.

When you compare yourself to someone else, you are doing yourself a disservice because in so doing, you are negating a very important truth: you are unique and nobody can be you better than you can.

Take the example of comparing your everyday looks to those of your friend who posts amazing images on Facebook or Instagram. When you do this, out of an erroneous conclusion that your friend is faring better than you are, you erode your confidence. If nothing else, take from this book the attitude of uniqueness: you are unique. You have unique strengths and weaknesses. If you play to your strengths and work on your weaknesses, you will be unstoppable.

NOTE: Scientific research has actually concluded that comparing yourself to other people actually breeds envy and a negative self-image. Learn more this and this resource.

9: Desensitize Yourself to Rejection

Oftentimes, our resolve not to do something comes from the fear of rejection or judgment. For instance, out of the fear of rejection, a single man will talk himself out of approaching and flirting with women. Out of the fear of rejection and perhaps judgment, many of us shy away from commitments that thrust us into the limelight with public speaking being a great example.

Eleanor Roosevelt once noted that, *"No one can make you feel inferior without your consent."* Given, since a lack of confidence is the existence of an inferior complex, it is easy to conclude that Eleanor's advice is contextual. That may be but when you desensitize yourself to rejection, things take a drastic turn and your self-image stops depending on other peoples' opinions of you.

Embark on a 100-day challenge. For instance, if you are skeptical of your ability to engage strangers in conversation, for 100-days, talk to strangers. Approach them with the understanding that you will not be everyone's cup of tea: some will reject you and your approach, which is OK.

This strategy is one of the most effective ways to build self-confidence all the while building a new skill and having fun at the same time.

10: Set Boundaries and Become more Assertive

Inasmuch as confidence is a firm belief in your abilities, it also relates to your ability to voice your opinion as well as to say NO to others as well as yourself. Remember the lessons Harvey Forbes Fierstein aimed to teach when he said, *"Never be bullied into silence. Never allow anyone to make you a victim. Accept no one's definition of your life, but define yourself."*

Setting boundaries is all about teaching others—and to some degree, yourself—what you can and cannot tolerate. Without boundaries, things like emotional and physical abuse and people using you, which BTW, erodes your confidence, are likely to be rampant in your life.

Assertiveness, the ability to stand up for yourself and what you believe in, is a great way to build confidence. Since cultivating assertiveness requires you to take stock of your emotions, strengths, weaknesses, and what you want and need, it gives you courage to stand up for what you want and need and to express your opinion. Courage and a lack of self-confidence cannot inhabit the same vessel.

Chapter 2: 6 Foolproof Health Actions that Effectively Improve Your Self-confidence

If you are not comfortable with (or in) your body, the lack of comfort is likely to breed an inferior complex that causes a dip in your confidence. On the other hand, when you OWN your body and everything about it, your confidence soars and you feel good about yourself.

This chapter discusses physical health actions you can take to improve your level of self-confidence:

11: Get Enough Sleep

A lack of adequate sleep is a recipe for disaster and a diminishing level of self-confidence. Think of it this way. Sleep is the body's way of recuperating and rejuvenating after the demands of the day.

Sleep deprivation makes you dumber, kills your sex drive, causes depression, ages your skin rapidly, leads to weight gain, and guess what, it can also lead to impaired judgement.

When you get enough sleep, you avoid all the above and in so doing, maintain a healthy frame of mind that allows you to remain positive and confident of your ability to take on whatever you have planned for the day.

Moreover, getting enough sleep replenishes your willpower reserve. Willpower is super important to you as you work towards building your confidence because in essence, willpower, is a sense of self-control over self. When you can exert more control over yourself, your confidence soars to heights never before imagined.

12: Adopt A Healthy Diet

You are what you eat. If you eat junk food, in addition to feeling bad about your body, your choice of food will also have a detrimental effect on other aspects of your life such as your sleep and productivity. That food affects our mood and behavior is not new; in fact, the field has fascinating research findings that relate food to our mental health and body image.

To improve your self-esteem (body image), it is essential to take charge of your dietary choices because as you may know, food can help boost your mood, reduce anxiety, and in some cases, even make you feel better and good about yourself.

Here, we only have on secret: aim for a healthy, nutrient rich diet drawn from all types of foods. Eat sufficient amounts of carbs, proteins, and fats. Complex carbs are of specific importance here because they stimulate the production of serotonin, a hormone related to increased relaxation, positivity, and therefore confidence.

Limit your intake of caffeinated drinks, sugar, and alcohol and in their place, eat foods rich in vitamin B and D, selenium, and omega-3 fatty acids.

13: Exercise

You probably saw this one coming from a mile away. Yes, exercise is one of the most effective confidence-building actions there is. Since self-confidence is a product of your beliefs, it makes sense that exercising and pushing yourself harder in the process is effective at building self-confidence.

Another aspect of this is the changes that come from

exercising. As you exercise, your body changes. For instance, the love handles start disappearing, your butt and thighs firm up, and the flab under your arms disappears. As you can imagine, seeing these changes can have a positive effect on your self-esteem.

Exercising also leaves you with a feeling of elation, of prideful victory of what you have managed to achieve. Exercise also triggers the release of feel good hormones; this is why after an exercise session, you feel a sense of accomplishment and joy.

14: Drink Enough Water

Does water really have any effect on your level of confidence? The answer is yes; here is why.

Drinking water has many scientifically proven benefits. For instance, scientists believe that drinking enough water can have a dramatic effect on your weight loss endeavor or journey. "How does water and weight loss relate to self-confidence," you ask. Well, when you feel great about your body, your confidence also grows exponentially.

The other aspect of this is the fact that drinking enough water improves your mood. When you drink water, you feel refreshed, an effect that also permeates to the mind where it refreshes the mind too, thus improving your mental state.

Moreover, scientific research has shown that dehydration shrinks brain tissues. When you stay hydrated, in addition to thinking clearly, you also promote brain health and ensure that your brain is refreshed and working at its best capacity. As you can imagine, when you feel focused on your goals and aims for the day, your belief in your capabilities is also likely to improve.

15: Positive Body Talk

We often concentrate on the things we hate about our bodies and rarely concentrate on how amazing our bodies truly are. Just as positive thinking and positive self-talk can help you on a mental level, they can also help you experience a sense of confidence in what your body can do for you.

Take to the habit of appreciating your body. At the start, end, or at several instances during the day, even as you notice the extra flab and "perceived" deformities, notice just how capable your body truly is. Appreciate the fact that you have enough energy for all your aims and undertakings. When you look in the mirror, focus more on the capabilities of your body and what it helps you achieve in your daily life. Amy Flowers, PhD says we should all start seeing our bodies as allies instead of enemies. Obviously, when you feel good about your body, your self-image and self-esteem improve.

16: Practice Self-care

Parker Palmer, an American author, once noted that, *"Self-care is never a selfish act. It is simply good stewardship of the only gift I have, the gift I was put on earth to offer to others."*

Since your self-confidence is a combination of factors such as your social, health, and emotional wellbeing, when you fail to care for your physical and mental health and wellbeing, you end up hating yourself—perhaps your physique or state of mind—, which ends up eroding your level of self-confidence.

On the other hand, when you make time for yourself, and use this time creatively, perhaps to exercise the mind and the body, to sleep, or to meditate, you start feeling great about yourself and in so doing, your confidence starts improving.

Chapter 3: 7 Highly Actionable Body Language Actions For Improved Self-Confidence

Body language forms a large percentage of how we communicate. Unfortunately, many of us concentrate on verbal communication. Because of it, we use body language cues that erode our confidence as well as confidence in what we are saying.

The following body language hacks will help improve your confidence rapidly:

17: Moderate your Speech

When we get nervous, we speak out of sorts, fast and sometimes incomprehensibly. To experience an immediate jolt of confidence, choose to speak leisurely and in a clear voice. In fact, speaking slowly actually clarifies your speech and in effect, makes you sound confident.

The postulation here is not absurd. When you speak hurriedly, you show people one of two things: that you lack personal trust, or that you are in a hurry to end the conversation—perhaps because you are nervous.

When you slow down, in addition to clarifying your speech, it also gives you an aura of confidence that leads the people or person you are in conversation with to conclude that since you are taking great care to moderate what you say and how you say it, you are someone worth listening to and the attention. Knowing you are commanding someone's undivided attention is a massive confidence boost.

18: Open Up Your Body

We can classify body language into two classes: open and closed body language. When you close off your body, you appear unconfident, dull, and defensive; you turn away people that would have otherwise loved to engage you in a conversation.

On the other hand, when you open up your body language, which is to mean you adopt relaxed body language cues, you appear confident and welcome, as someone who has nothing to fear and is open for the business of conversation and creating mutually interesting connections.

A hack you can use here is to take up as much as possible—of course accounting for context. The logic here is that because they know their boundaries and are assertive people, confident people do not shy away from claiming as much space as they need to feel comfortable.

19: Speak from the Belly

Speaking from the belly is one of the most invaluable body language hacks you will find in this and other self-confidence building books. Thanks to our wiring, our subconscious automatically associates speaking from the belly with confidence, competence, and authority.

Because most of us speak from the throat, when you speak from the belly, you sound confident to others as well as to yourself. Speaking from the belly helps you project a confident voice and aura. As is the case with learning other skills, learning how to do so effectively takes time and consistent practice. The steps, however, are relatively uncomplicated and thus doable in as little as five minutes a day.

20: Dress to Impress

As we noted earlier, how you feel and what you think about your looks greatly influences your self-image and more importantly, your self-confidence. For a jolt of confidence and a positive body image, dress in a way that leaves you feeling good about yourself and that therefore improves your self-confidence.

Make sure your grooming habits are on point and that you dress in clothes that complement you. Appear clean and smell nice. The more well groomed you are, the more confident you will feel.

21: Mind your Posture

Your posture is very communicative. When you are unsure, you tend to walk with your shoulders rolled or hunched forwards, head and eyes down, using small steps that appear as if you are afraid of the ground breaking apart and swallowing you whole. Such a posture is detrimental to your confidence.

Get into the habit of watching your body language, your posture especially, and when you catch a slump in it, straighten yourself out. For instance, because of the sitting nature of modern day societies, many of us tend to slum into our chairs, a fact that affects our standing posture too.

Whether you are sitting or standing, train your mind to notice such slumps and your use of body language, and to make the necessary changes. For posture, all you have to do is straighten out. Worth noting here is that we did not say to straighten out rigidly; whether you are sitting or standing, aim to maintain the natural curvature of your spine. Your back and self-confidence will thank you immensely for it.

Here, the most important hacks are to stand tall with your shoulders straight and your chin and head held up. Another hack is to tighten your core—not stiffen—for doing so will make you appear taller and therefore more open and confident. In addition to this, stand with your feet a bit further apart—shoulder width apart to be precise—and if in a conversation, use your hands, body, and other forms of gestures to accentuate your communication.

22: Adopt Power Poses

Led by Amy Cuddy, body language researchers at Harvard University unearthed the existence of specific body poses called power poses that when adopted, immediately improve your confidence by a significant margin.

Check the image below:

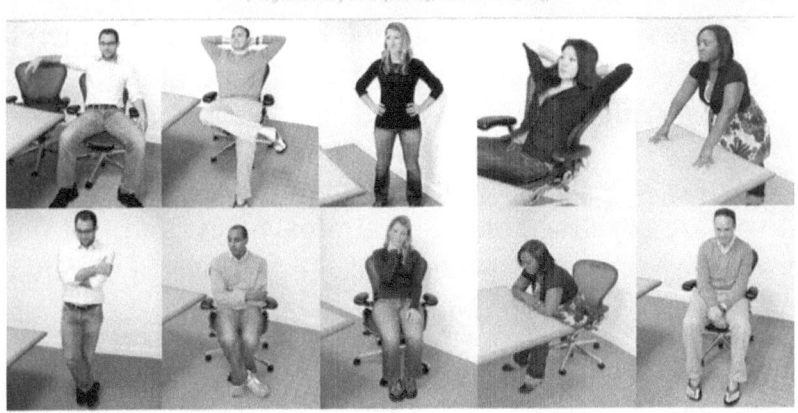

"High Power" body language (top row)
vs.
"Low Power" body language (bottom row)
(Images courtesy of Amy Cuddy, Harvard University)

Amy and her team of researchers noted that by adopting high power body language, study participants reported feeling happier and more confident. On the other hand, participants who adopted low power body language cues reported feeling less confident.

From their research, Amy and her team noted something very peculiar: that standing in the wonder woman pose, standing long and tall, chest out, and hands at akimbo, made participants feel an immediate jolt of confidence. If you adopt the wonder woman pose for even as little as 2 minutes, it will have a dramatic effect on your confidence levels.

23: Smile, Maintain Eye Contact, and Be Interested

The human mind translates a smile to mean attractiveness, openness, and trustworthiness. When you smile, you appear welcoming and sure of your place in the world. Here is a real-world experiment for you.

Whip out a pencil or pen and stick it between your jaws for a minute or two. When you do this, you will quickly notice that because the act stimulates a smile, you will gradually start feeling better. There is a scientific reason for this: in addition to infusing your spirit with warmth and confidence, smiling also triggers the release of feel good hormones and is therefore very beneficial for your health. As we have noted severally, when you feel good, you feel confident.

Maintaining eye contact, on the other hand, communicates that you are attentive, engaged, approachable, and truthful. A lack of eye contact can communicate a sense of deceit and make you appear less confident.

Maintaining eye contact is contextual and yes, too much eye contact is a thing of which communicates a level of aggressiveness. Also avoid staring, most people find it uncomfortable to a point where incessant staring activates someone's flight-or-fight response.

The most effective way to maintain eye contact is to do so

covertly. When engaged in a conversation, maintain direct eye contact at several instances and in the other times, map out a triangle between the person's eyes and the bridge of his or her nose. When you do break eye contact, no matter how momentarily, avoid looking down and instead, look to the side.

As for interest, the best way to use your body to communicate an internal and external sense of confidence is to give your conversation partner your full attention and to show interest. When you give a person your interest and attention, you automatically become engaged, and in so doing, it communicates that you are comfortable with whom you are and free from the need to talk about yourself incessantly, which as you may have guessed, is normally a tactic we use to hide our insecurities.

Chapter 4: 5 Super Powerful Confidence Habits You Should Adopt

Like success, confidence is a habit whose mastery requires consistent practice. Only by habitually practicing self-confidence as a daily discipline can you master it. While you should make the actions we have discussed thus far part of your daily routine, also adopt the following habits that will help you inculcate self-confidence:

24: Habitual Reading

Other than the fact that it is a self-development strategy, reading is an effective confidence building habit because when you adopt it and continuously do it, it becomes a sort of therapy that gets you out of your head and therefore out of the negative thought pattern loop that breeds an inferiority complex and a wanting level of self-discipline. In addition, the more you read the more you learn so much and this knowledge actually makes you feel confident especially when interacting with people who are talking about topics you have read.

While you are free to read whatever tickles your fancy, especially get into the habit of reading motivational, self-help content that helps better your life. Especially get into the habit of reading at a specific time of day—perhaps in the morning. This is very beneficial because it will routinize your life, which, when you know what to expect from your day, will leave you feeling immensely capable.

25: Strength Training

As noted earlier, any form of exercise is an effective confidence-building conduit. Strength training is a form of exercising. However, unlike other forms of exercise, working out using weights has standout confidence building effects.

For starters, strength training, especially when you are pushing yourself to the brink of exhaustion, you effectively manage to get out of your mind and to let go off all manner of tension and stress. Getting out of your mind helps you to break the internal negative loop that leads to decreased self-confidence.

26: Set Daily Goals and Take Positive Actions

Goals are the most important aspects of a value-driven life. When your life is devoid of goals, it means you have no direction and because of this lack, you cannot be assertive enough to be decisive with yourself and others.

When you get into the habit of setting clear goals for yourself and then keep yourself accountable—to yourself and to someone else—by tracking your progress on a daily basis, seeing your growth immensely stimulates your self-confidence and your motivation to keep going until you master specific areas of your life.

Taking positive action consistently is actually how you buff up your skill repertoire and how you become more confident in the different areas that make up your life. For instance, by taking daily actions towards practicing the strategies in this guide, you gradually increase your self-confidence until it becomes impermeable. Remember that confidence is a habit, not a state of being.

This guide especially urges you to challenge yourself every day by attempting something that scares you.

27: Journal

Journaling is a scientifically proven way to a better self-image—and therefore, we can postulate more confidence.

When you get into the habit of writing down your thoughts and about your day, you immediately quiet your monkey mind and above that, you stop the negative thought patterns that breed a negative mindset and a discolored self-image.

As you take up journaling, whether in a special journal or in a notebook, especially journal about what you feel (your emotions), your capabilities, and your progressive approach to your goals.

Reading an account of how you completed a 10k run on Sunday will give you the motivation you need to push through the week with vigor.

28: Practice Gratitude

Be grateful for every blessing in your life. Be grateful for the fact that you are consistently working towards being a better person. Be grateful that you have the will and the ability to work on yourself.

While your confidence may yet be where you want it to be, you are actively working towards improving it, which is something to give thanks for having. What gratitude does is shift your mindset from a lacking one to one that sees opportunities and growth at every turn. When you attune yourself to this, your self-confidence automatically soars.

Conclusion

We have come to the end of the book. Thank you for reading and congratulations for reading until the end.

I trust it has proven itself a true ally in your quest to become a more confident person. Implement what you have learned for positive action taken consistently is the secret to all achievements.

If you found the book valuable, can you recommend it to others? One way to do that is to post a review on Amazon.

Click here to leave a review for this book on Amazon!

Thank you and good luck!

www.ingramcontent.com/pod-product-compliance
Lightning Source LLC
Chambersburg PA
CBHW030600220526
45463CB00007B/3130